All The Great Things About TURNING

35

ISBN 978-1547218615